The Thriving Woman's Guide to Job Interviews:

6 Steps to Your Best Job Interview Ever

Kim Buck, M.B.A.

The Thriving Woman's Guide to Job Interviews:
6 Steps to Your Best Job Interview Ever
Kim Buck, M.B.A.

Published by The Catalyst Group International Inc.
4 Selkirk Dr SW Calgary, Alberta T2W0M2 Canada
403-255-3235

All rights reserved. No part of this book may be reproduced by any mechanical, photographic or electronic process, or in the form of phonographic recording; nor may it be stored in a retrieval system, transmitted, or otherwise be copied for public or private use other than for "fair use" as brief quotations embodied in articles and reviews without permission in writing from The Catalyst Group International Inc.

Copyright © 2013 by Kim Buck
First Edition, 2013

Published in Canada

ISBN: 978-0-9739939-5-0

CONTENTS

About the Author
Acknowledgement
Disclaimer

INTRODUCTION	9
SECTION ONE: Before the Interview	13
STEP 1: Research the Company You Are Interviewing With	15
STEP 2: Your Appearance	21
STEP 3: Preparing For the Interview	27
A. Set Your Intention	27
B. Review Your Resume	31
C. Identify Your Strengths	37
D. Identify Your Weaknesses	41
E. Behavior Descriptive Interview Questions	49
F. Prepare Questions to Ask in the Interview	53
G. What is Your Vision For Your Career?	57
H. Why Should We Hire You?	61
I. Why are You Interested in This Position?	63
J. What is Your Current Salary or Hourly Wage?	65
K. Prepare Your List of References	69
L. Prepare Your Handshake	73
STEP 4: What to Bring to the Interview and What Not to Bring to the Interview	75
SECTION TWO: The Interview	79
STEP 5: The Interview	83
SECTION THREE: After the Interview	97
STEP 6 After the Interview	99

SECTION FOUR: Simple Energy Tips	101
FINAL WORD	111
REFERENCES	114
Index	115

About the Author

Kim Buck, M.B.A., a Success Coach and catalyst, is the founder of Are You Willing to Be Seen? Coaching and is the author of *The Thriving Woman's Guide to*™ series. She has over 10 years of experience in the field of Recruiting. She has experience in Executive Search, Corporate Recruiting, IT Recruiting and IT Account Management. She has recruited for all levels in a organization and has interviewed thousands of candidates. She now coaches women on how to be successful with job changes, career changes and how to have their work be seen and acknowledged so they receive the recognition and promotion they deserve. For information see www.areyouwillingtobeseen.com.

ACKNOWLEDGEMENT

I received support and encouragement for this book from several magnificent people. I would like to express my gratitude and appreciation to:

Wendy Buck for being the catalyst of this book and for her thoughtful suggestions and publishing insights.

Mark Giovanetto, my beautiful husband, for believing that *The Thriving Woman's Guide to*™ series is important and for the daily encouragement to bring this book to completion.

Penny Giovanetto for her insightful editing of this book and for her excitement for future *The Thriving Woman's Guide to*™ titles.

Colleen Pilling for her thorough proofreading and enthusiastic feedback as well as her support and encouragement from the beginning.

Wayne Pilling for sharing Colleen Pilling's enthusiasm and for diligently proofreading a book dedicated to women's success.

DISCLAIMER

This book is designed to provide information on preparing yourself for an interview. It is sold with the understanding that the publisher and author are not engaged in rendering legal or other professional services. If legal or other expert assistance is required, the services of a competent professional should be sought.

It is not the purpose of this manual to reprint all the information that is otherwise available to job seekers, but instead to complement, amplify and supplement other texts. You are urged to read all the available material, learn as much as possible about interviews, and tailor the information to your individual needs.

Job interviewing is an individual process and no one process is the best way for all job candidates. Every effort has been made to make this manual as complete and as accurate as possible. However, there may be mistakes, both typographical and in content. Therefore, this text should be used only as a general guide and not as the ultimate source of job interview preparation.

The purpose of this manual is to educate and entertain. The author and The Catalyst Group International Inc. shall have neither liability nor responsibility to any person or entity with respect to any loss or damage caused, or alleged to have been caused, directly or indirectly, by the information contained in this book.

If you do not wish to be bound by the above, you may return this book to the publisher for a full refund.

INTRODUCTION

I used to work in the field of Recruiting. I have over 10 years experience recruiting people. I started out in Executive Search then I moved to Corporate Recruiting which was followed by Technical Recruiting and Account Management. I have interviewed for every level in an organization and I have interviewed thousands of people. Now I coach women on achieving success with interviews, job changes, promotions and career changes. My purpose is to help women see themselves as powerful contributors and I love to help women move forward in their careers.

There are lots of books out there on interviews and how to interview. The vast majority of these books are written from the view of providing you with a standard answer to the interviewer's questions. Many of these books don't really prepare you for the interview. They simply scare you before you get there. As well, these books don't teach you, as a woman, how to manage your energy so that you can thrive in your interview. In addition to prepping you for the actual interview, this guide will help you understand how to manage your energy with simple do's and don'ts so that the interview process doesn't activate a destructive level of fear in you.

I am always amazed at how unprepared people are for interviews. You should always be prepared for your interview. It will set you apart from the rest of the candidates being interviewed. Most people think that the actual interview is the key part of the process. Actually, most of what happens in the interview will be based on the steps that you take before you get to the interview. There are six steps, and if you follow them, you will have a successful interview and shine above the other candidates.

What is an Interview?

Before I get into the 6 steps, I want to cover what an interview is. Interviews are scary for a lot of people. They don't need to be. An interview is a conversation you have with someone who is interested in your background and who has invited you to come in and meet with them. Note the key parts of this:

> You are meeting with someone who is interested in meeting you.
>
> You are invited to meet with this person.
>
> This person wants to know more about you.

This person is going to ask you to tell them about yourself.

You are presented with the opportunity to share your experience, knowledge and background with this person.

Since this is a conversation, it provides you with an opportunity to learn more about the company.

When you think of an interview this way, it will be a lot less intimidating.

What Are Generally Accepted Interview Expectations?

A lot of what the interviewer bases his or her decision on in the interview is how he or she feels about you. This feeling comes from many factors, some the person is consciously aware of and some the person is subconsciously aware of. The subconscious awareness is the feeling the interviewer is getting of you and from you. The key to being successful in an interview is to activate feelings of trust in your interviewer. Trust is created through subconscious cues and biochemistry. It is also created through certain generally accepted expectations being met.

All places of work have generally accepted expectations for behavior and your interview is no different. Regardless of the type of job or level of job you are applying for, your interview is a business meeting. In North America, there are standards of behavior for interview candidates that are understood and expected. These are generally accepted interview expectations and they are mentioned throughout this book. When you meet these expectations, you build trust. When you don't meet these expectations, you start to build distrust. These generally accepted interview expectations may be different in other parts of the world.

SECTION ONE:

Before the Interview

STEP 1:

Research the Company You Are Interviewing With

Before you go for your interview, research the company you are meeting with. Everyone tells you to do this. Most people don't really know what type of information they need to be looking for or how that information is relevant to you and the hiring process.

Start out with a Google search on the company. If the company you are interviewing with is a public company (the company has shares that trade on a stock exchange) look at annual reports. Find out:

How long the company has been in business.

Key areas of business the company focuses on.

Who some of their main competitors are.

How big the company is in terms of revenue.

How many employees the company has.

Some of the challenges the company is facing.

Whether the company has been growing or declining over the last few years.

Read some of the company's tweets. See what other people are tweeting about the company and their products/services. See what is happening on their Facebook page. Look at their Pinterest page. Research some key employees on LinkedIn. Even if this is the only company in the town where you live, find out more about it. You will impress your interviewer with your knowledge, especially if the interviewer asks if you know anything about the company. You want to be able to say that you know more about it than just your friend works there and likes it.

Now take the information you have gathered and see how your experience, knowledge and background would help solve one of their problems or see if you can identify a problem that the company is experiencing that management might not even be aware of. Take a high level view of this information. For example, what does it mean to you that people on Twitter are complaining about a certain aspect of a product? What does this mean to the company? Or, as a candidate, what was appealing about the company website, Pinterest page, or Facebook page? What made you cringe when you read this information? Allow yourself to tap into your intuition for answers with this. You might even come up with the most valuable solution to a problem that the company doesn't even know it has.

When you are gathering your information on the company, keep asking yourself the following question, "Hmm, I wonder how my experience, knowledge and background would be valuable here?" The "Hmm, I wonder" part is really important. When you ask a question this way, you tap into your right brain, which is your creative, intuitive side of your brain. Don't answer this question by thinking about it. Just ask the question and allow an answer to come forward. Your interviewer will likely ask you this question in your interview and you want to have an answer ready. If you ask the question of yourself and allow an answer to come through, you will have an answer that will surprise you in a positive way and it will be much better than the answer you would get if you forced it by thinking about it. Allow your intuitive side to assist you in your interview preparation.

You can also ask your friends and family members how your experience, knowledge and background would be a benefit to this company. Make sure you only ask people who want the best for you. Your supporters see you in a way that you might not see yourself. They will likely mention projects, accomplishments, ideas and successes you have had that would be relevant to this position that you might discount or feel are unimportant.

Most people, if they do research on a company, go into an interview with facts about the company but not with an understanding of how their experience, knowledge and background ties in with this information and how it would benefit the organization.

Don't beat yourself up if you aren't able to piece together how the information you gathered could be useful in presenting yourself as the best candidate for the position. Remember, the information available is only a glimpse of what is going on at the hiring company. There may not be enough information to identify their problems or solutions. As well, you may be interviewing for a position that the interviewer wouldn't be expecting you to have insights about.

If the company you are interviewing with is a privately held company (owned privately by an individual or group of people), you may not be able to find out much information. That is okay. You can go into your interview and mention that you did a search on the company but you couldn't find any information. Public companies are required by law to publicly share information on the company. Private companies are not required to share any information. It is important, though, to still ask yourself the question, "Hmm, I wonder how my experience, knowledge and background would be valuable here?" Regardless of whether the hiring company is publicly held or privately held, you still want to identify how you would be valuable to them.

As you are doing this part of your research, in addition to asking yourself how you would be valuable to the hiring company, identify what is appealing about this position and this company. Why are you interested in being hired on with this company? If you are currently unemployed, and it is the only company hiring, then the answer is pretty simple. You want work. If it isn't the only company hiring, then why this one? If you aren't sure 'why this company?' then ask the question, "Hmm, I wonder what appeals to me about this position and this company?" Allow an answer to come to you.

As part of your research, go to where your position will likely be. If it is an office position, go to the building where the office is located and hang out in the lobby for a half hour at the start of the day or at lunch or at the end of the day. Observe how most people are dressed. Even though you won't have specific information on your intended company, this will give you a general idea of your company. You will see how most people in the office building are dressed. Write down your overall impression. If you are applying for a retail position, go to the store and see what the employees are wearing and how busy it is. If everyone is wearing black, make a note of that. If your work requires you to wear a uniform, you can skip the part about seeing how people are dressed. This part obviously won't be relevant to you. Regardless, wherever your job will be, go there and hang out for a bit. Get an overall impression of the work environment. Be casual about this. You aren't stalking people.

STEP 2:

Your Appearance

There are several aspects to your appearance and all of these points are important. Your appearance and being dressed appropriately are part of the generally accepted interview expectations people have in the workplace. When you meet these expectations, people feel comfortable with you. When you don't meet these expectations, people feel uncomfortable with you.

CLOTHING
Now that you have researched the company for your interview, dress to the level of what you observed or better. For any position above entry level, you should wear a suit or at least wear a jacket with your pants or skirt. Keep the color toned down. Black, navy, other shades of darker blues, brown or camel are suitable colors for women's suits. You want the suit to be the canvas to profile you. You don't want the suit to take the lead. Even if the company you are interviewing

with is a very casual workplace and everyone there always wears jeans and a tee-shirt, wearing a suit to the interview will impress the interviewer. Remember, this person might be meeting with 5 to 10 candidates on the day that you are interviewed. You want to stand out in that person's mind for all the right reasons. If you don't own a suit or you really don't feel comfortable in a suit, wear the best clothing that you have. Keep it simple with a white shirt and pressed pants or a knee-length or longer skirt. Don't wear anything short, tight or revealing unless you are interviewing for a position that requires that type of clothing like a serving position at certain restaurants. Remember, you are interviewing for a job, not going out to a nightclub.

DO NOT WEAR JEANS! I have interviewed and recruited for all levels of positions in organizations. If you walked in wearing jeans, I simply wouldn't hire you. If you wear jeans to an interview, it says to me that you aren't all that interested in the position. Even if you are interviewing for a mechanics position or construction or something similar or an IT position where jeans are always worn, show respect for your interviewer and wear something more dressed-up than jeans.

SHOES
Make sure your shoes are polished. Dirt, dust, and scuff marks make it look like you don't care. A lot of people notice the state of your shoes.

> Wear dress shoes.
>
> Don't wear sandals, flip flops, Birkenstocks, slingbacks, or runners.

LOOK POLISHED
Clean your nails. Dirty nails on others make people feel uncomfortable.

Don't wear any monster fake nails. No matter how much you love them, unless you are applying for a position at a nail salon, you want it to appear that you are able to work. Some people see long, fake nails as tacky and that will negatively impact your overall impression.

Don't wear wild nail polish colors or bling on your nails. This is distracting. You want your appearance to be in the background and your experience to be in the spotlight.

Go easy on the makeup. If you normally wear a lot, wear less for the interview. A lot of makeup is distracting and sometimes it makes it harder for people to take you seriously. Remember, you are interviewing for a job, not going out to the bar. If you don't normally wear any makeup, wear a bit for the interview. It will make you look more alive and polished. If you don't know how to apply it, go to any cosmetic counter for a free lesson. Most cosmetic counters will generally give you some free sample products for you to take home.

Get a hair cut before your interview. Messy or unkempt hair is often one of the first things someone will notice about you. People can make a snap decision about you from your hair. Whatever your hair length, make sure it won't fall in your face during the interview. And, don't play with your hair in the interview, even if this is your nervous habit. If you aren't sure if this is your nervous habit, ask friends or family members if this is the case.

Don't wear a lot of jewelry. It is distracting. This isn't a fashion show. It is a job interview. Keep your jewelry to a minimum and keep it simple.

FRAGRANCE
Don't wear perfume to the interview. Even if you feel you can't get through the day without it, don't wear it. You don't know whether your interviewer is bothered or reactive to perfume. I am highly sensitive to scents and when I meet with someone who has perfume on, I simply want to say hi and bye at the same time. I don't

want to compromise my health because you like your fragrance. And, if your fragrance has caused me a migraine, I am no longer interested or focused on what you are saying. I simply want to go home. Do, however, wear deodorant/antiperspirant. You are going to be nervous and you are going to sweat. You don't want to smell like you just worked out.

Hiring is done by people. These people could have all kinds of judgments that may be unfair but they hold the cards in the job hiring process. If you have a highly specialized skillset and many companies are competing for you, then you can get away with more in an interview. I suspect if you are reading this book then that isn't the case for you. You want to give yourself the greatest advantage that you can in your interview and following these points will give you that advantage.

STEP 3:

Preparing For the Interview

A. Set Your Intention

It is really important to set an intention as you prepare for your interview. Intention is an active process. It is full of power. An intention is a clear statement of what you desire to experience and how you desire to experience it. It is strongest if you write it down but saying it out loud will work as well. An intention is a directive to yourself and the universe that says you desire to receive something in the way you desire to receive it. It is a powerful form of thought energy.

Be clear on your intention for this interview preparation and for the outcome of your interview. What do you desire to experience as you prepare for your interview? Do you desire to come away from this process with a greater understanding of who you are and what your successes have been? Do you desire to go through this process with ease? Do you desire it to be hard? Do you resent having to go through this process? Do you desire to feel strong, powerful and confident when you go to your interview? Be clear on what you desire to experience with this interview preparation process and how you desire to experience it. Write this down. Don't allow your thoughts to stray from this intention. Be committed to this intention as you go through the interview preparation process. As an example, your intention for your interview preparation might be something like this, "It is my intention to go through this interview preparation with ease. I allow myself to use this process as a way to feel powerful and confident. With grace, I explore my past successes and identify how my skills, knowledge and abilities will move me forward."

What do you desire as your outcome of your interview? Do you want to be offered the job? Do you want to find out if this company is a fit for you? Do you desire to be paid more than you currently are? Claim your right to state your desire and be specific with this. Write this down. Stay focused on this intention as you go through your interview.

Thoughts are energy. Everything in the universe is made of energy. Your thoughts are generated from your spirit and can have a profound influence on people around you. Your thoughts are continually radiating from your body. They act like tuning forks sending out a vibration that gets picked up by someone who is tuned to the same frequency. What if your thought was, 'I don't deserve to get this job' or 'They aren't going to hire me' or 'The other candidates are better suited for this job'? Your interviewer will be picking up on this even if he or she isn't fully aware of this. Focus on what you desire from your interview.

STEP 3:

Preparing For the Interview

B. Review Your Resume

Be prepared for the interview. This sounds like common sense but you would be surprised how many people come to an interview unprepared. Being prepared for your interview is a generally accepted expectation interviewers have of candidates. Being prepared builds trust. Being unprepared creates distrust.

Review Your Resume
It is important to review your resume before your interview.

> Know relevant dates. When did you start and end each job?
>
> What were your key responsibilities in each job?
>
> What were your key successes in each job?

What were you most proud of with each job?

What was your greatest accomplishment in each job?

What was your greatest challenge in each job?

What did you like most about each job?

What did you dislike about each job?

Why did you leave each job?

What was a typical day like at each job? A typical month?

Who did you report to at each job?

You want this information to flow when you are sharing it with your interviewer. You don't want to be stumbling over start dates or the order of each job. It is easy when you are nervous to get scattered in your thinking, especially if you haven't prepared yourself to talk about your work history. I know this sounds ridiculous but you would be surprised how dates jumble together when you are nervous and you haven't taken the time to review your resume. As well, when you take the time to review your resume, it helps build confidence. As you review each job and think about your successes, you may think of something you accomplished in certain positions that may not otherwise come to mind. Allow yourself to reflect on what a great job you did and the value you brought to each position.

Just as an aside, update your resume regularly. We generally only update our resume when we are applying for a new position. When we do this, we often miss out on capturing many of the successes we had along the way. It is often difficult when you are writing a resume to remember all the good things that you were part of. A client of mine is interested in moving to a higher level position in a different organization. She has been working on some interesting online learning projects for her current employer. I asked her if she is keeping a list of the projects she has worked on and she said no. She said it simply hadn't occurred to her to keep a list of her projects. I asked her if a prospective employer would find her experience in implementing a wide range of online learning courses to be valuable and would this increase her value to the prospective company. She agreed that this would indeed be useful and it would be a great way to set herself apart from other candidates.

It is very helpful to keep a running log or list of what you accomplished as you do it. Keep a list of processes you implemented that made your work flow much better. Track the 'cool' projects you were part of or were responsible for. Capture how you saved your current employer money. Write down the ideas you came up with and shared that have been implemented in other areas of your company. Even if your day seems very routine and you feel like there isn't anything special that you did week to week over the last while, I am willing to bet that there were many things that you did that would be appealing to your future employer. Keeping track of all of these will do two things. First, it will build confidence in you. You will have a record of success that is factual. It will help you see the value you have added to your current and past employers. Second, it will give you a list of successes that you can share with your interviewer. Every time you implement a process, begin a project, finish a project, or find a different and better way of doing some aspect of your job, write it down. Get into the habit of capturing your successes and accomplishments. You also want to capture any committees you have led or worked on and what your contributions were. This includes the social club.

If you had some failures in certain positions, allow yourself to ask the questions, "Hmm, I wonder what I could have done differently there to make it more successful? Hmm, I wonder what was right about this position? Hmm, I wonder what I learned from this?" As I mentioned earlier in the section on researching the company, the 'Hmm, I wonder' part of these questions helps you get into the right side of your brain, which is the intuitive side of your brain. Allow these answers to come forward without forcing some preconceived view on them. Self-awareness is really valuable. If something didn't go well and you learned from it, this has tremendous value. Sharing with your interviewer that you learned something really important about yourself adds to your credibility. *Important point here* – you don't want to dwell on your past struggles or challenges. You really want to identify and focus on the successes you have had in past positions and simply have an awareness of why some things didn't go well.

STEP 3:

Preparing For the Interview

C. Identify Your Strengths

Before going to your interview, identify and understand what your strengths are. The interviewer will likely ask you about them. You need to have an answer for this. If you aren't sure what your strengths are, I have a few suggestions for you to determine them.

First, ask the question, "Hmm, I wonder what my strengths are?" As mentioned earlier, the 'Hmm, I wonder' will get you into your creative, intuitive right brain and will allow answers to come through that you wouldn't access just by thinking about it. Write down what comes to mind.

Second, you can ask your friends and family to tell you what they see as your strengths. It is important to only ask those people who want you to be successful with this interview. Don't ask anyone who doesn't want the best for you. When you ask your supporters what your strengths are, it will give you a nice, and sometimes surprising and unexpected, idea of how others see you. They may mention things that you didn't really feel mattered but they found impressive. You could also ask previous supervisors/managers what they thought your strengths are. If you graduated recently, you could ask any of your instructors with whom you had interaction what they saw as your strengths and compile your list that way.

The third way to come up with your list of strengths is to look at the job description you will be interviewing for and highlight 3 or 4 key aspects of the position that you would like to focus on that you are good at. As an example, a client of mine was making a career change and she wanted to go in a new career direction. She had recently resigned from being an elementary school teacher and she needed a way to move from that role to a corporate position. She had identified 3 key skills that she excelled at and that she wanted to focus on in her next position. She decided that she excelled at planning, scheduling and organizing. She applied for a position that turned out to be a project management role, although it wasn't called that in the job posting. This client went into this project management interview saying that her strengths were planning, scheduling and organizing – perfect qualities for a project manager. She got the job.

Be sure that the strengths you mention are your actual strengths. If they aren't, and you somehow get this job, it won't take long before your manager realizes that you lied in the interview. You don't want to misrepresent yourself in an interview. Doing so can have serious, negative consequences.

STEP 3:

Preparing For the Interview

D. Identify Your Weaknesses

Next, identify your weaknesses. Usually an interviewer will ask you to list 3 or 4 weaknesses. Everyone has weaknesses. Generally, interview books will tell you to take a strength and turn it into a weakness. You could do this. However, I believe it is better to mention an actual weakness and explain what you are doing about it. Just to be clear here, you don't want to mention weaknesses that will prevent you from getting hired. You don't want to mention that you are always late or that you have no idea how to organize or prioritize your work or anything like that.

Here you want to mention behaviors that you are aware of that aren't supporting your highest version of yourself. Start out by asking yourself what traits you have that aren't pleasing to you. As an interesting way to identify these behaviors, ask friends and family members what they feel your weaknesses are and ask them why they feel that way. This will give you an interesting perspective on how these weaknesses impact others. If you hold the view that everything is about you, hearing how your behavior impacts others negatively might help you to become less self-involved. If you hold the view that everything is about others, hearing how your weaknesses make others feel sad for you might help you to understand that these behaviors aren't supporting your well-being. Only ask people who want the best for you. This isn't open season for others to dump all over you.

Generally speaking, I believe women have one or more of the following weaknesses: perfectionism, being a people-pleaser, being a multi-tasker and not owning your voice. These aren't character flaws but they are behaviors that undermine your greatness. I will discuss each one separately.

Most people think that perfectionism is a great quality and that it really shows that you care. In reality, perfectionism is a time-waster. You will never do anything perfectly and aiming for that is unproductive. It is also a way to procrastinate and it makes it difficult to get other important tasks completed. Perfectionism is a persistent loop that allows you to beat up on yourself and ultimately to be cruel to yourself. It is an expectation that is impossible to achieve and it keeps your fight or flight response always activated in your body. Aiming for perfection at work or in your personal life keeps you in a constant state of panic and activates the feeling that you are never good enough. If this is an area of struggle for you share that with your interviewer. Let the person know that you are working on being okay with things being good enough and that you are giving yourself permission to let go of this debilitating pattern.

Being a people-pleaser is a huge problem for women. It is exhausting and debilitating. It allows others to take advantage of us and manipulate us into doing things that we don't want to do or aren't good at doing. And, it leaves us without a knowing of who we really are. Setting boundaries is often difficult to do, especially at work. Companies often take advantage of the fact that employees are afraid of losing their jobs if they say no to something. If you are a people-pleaser - and quite frankly most women have been raised to be that - start out by setting boundaries in your personal life. As a woman, you have the right to live a life that pleases you and you have the right to establish the 'rules' by which other people will treat you.

As women, we often believe that we don't have the right to set boundaries. This isn't true. What is true is that we often don't want responsibility (or respond ability – the ability to respond to something) for our lives. A boundary is a limit. It says this is what I am willing to have in my life and this is what I am not willing to have in my life. At a subconscious level, everyone is constantly seeking limits. It is quite unsettling, at a subconscious level, to push and find no limit. This creates an anxiety that is hard to pinpoint the underlying cause. People perform best and are most calm within when there are parameters in place. Boundaries, or limits, allow people to feel safe. The lack of limits creates unease, dis-ease and possibly disease. The caveat to this, of course, is if the boundary is too tight and people feel they are being controlled. When starting to set boundaries, ask yourself these questions, "What pleases me? Does this person's behavior please me? Does this person's request please me? What would please me in this situation?" Once you ask these questions, you can start to establish limits. Start to establish limits with your kids. Establish limits with your friends. Establish limits with your partner. Establish limits with your colleagues at work. As you become better at setting boundaries, you will become more confident in every area of your life.

People will often say that having boundaries is selfish. How did establishing limits to what is acceptable to you become seen as selfish? Just because you no longer respond to every request you receive doesn't mean you are selfish. Perhaps requiring the person making the request to take care of the situation himself or herself will help that person step into his or her greatness. And, certainly telling someone that their behavior doesn't please you isn't selfish. You are not here on this planet to put up with everything that comes your way.

When you are sharing this at your interview and you say that one of your weaknesses is being a people-pleaser, share how you are establishing limits with others so that you don't burn out. Share that you realize how debilitating it has been for you to not have any boundaries. Explain to your interviewer that you understand how important it is for you to set limits so that you can always be at your best at work and that this is a work in progress for you because it is.

Being a multi-tasker is a weakness. First of all, it is an illusion that anyone can multi-task and if you believe you can, you are simply deluding yourself. The brain is not set up to do two tasks at one time. It simply isn't possible. We can only attend to one activity at a time. Pay attention to this and see if you can truly do two activities at the same time. Try to type a document and have a conversation. Or try to listen to what your colleague/child/partner/friend is saying while you are reading a text message. Or try to prepare your budget while you are thinking about what to cook for dinner. Or the next time you are texting and driving, pay attention to how much you are actually aware of what is going on outside your vehicle. It just can't happen. You will either end up doing one of the activities sufficiently to the exclusion of the other or you will do both very poorly.

Companies these days are saying that they are looking for multi-taskers. This is ridiculous. That person doesn't exist. Saying that you are one is a weakness. What companies really want is someone who has a high level of productivity, can organize and prioritize their work and who can be interrupted often and get back to the task at hand quickly and easily. Doing that is a strength, multi-tasking is a weakness.

When you try to multi-task, nothing you do is done well.

If you believe you are a multi-tasker, in your interview, share with your interviewer that you are a multi-tasker. If your interviewer asks why that is a weakness, share that you have spent your time trying to do several things at the same time and that you have come to realize that this is impossible because our brains can't do two tasks at the same time. Let your interviewer know that you are capable of completing lots of tasks quickly, you can prioritize your work and that you can be interrupted often and get refocused on the task at hand quickly and easily. Let the interviewer know that you have found doing one task at a time leads to increased efficiency and enables you to complete tasks to a high standard. Let your interviewer know that that is really what he or she is looking for and that you are that person. Just a note about this. Remember to be truthful. Don't state this if you find being interrupted upsetting, you can't prioritize your work well and you have a hard time getting back to the task at hand.

Not owning your voice is a real problem for women. We have been raised not to speak out and we have often learned early on that speaking out comes with negative consequences. The problem with this is that women have a lot of valuable insights to share and companies are missing out when women don't own their voice. I am not talking about being bitchy or saying something for the sake of saying something. No,

I am talking about sharing your ideas and insights and speaking up when something doesn't feel right. It also means to be confident in what you are speaking about and to have a knowing that you have a right to be heard. Not owning your own voice leaves you without a solid knowing of who you really are and it makes it difficult for others to develop a sense of trust in you. When you have confidence in what you are saying and a confidence in your right to be heard, others respond to that in a favorable way. If this is a struggle for you, let your interviewer know that you have been working on this and you are finding owning your own voice is becoming easier for you to do. Make sure you own your voice in the interview. Be clear, speak up and confidently share your background. Know that you have a right to be heard.

STEP 3:

Preparing For the Interview

E. Behavior Descriptive Interview Questions

Now that you have reviewed your resume and identified your strengths and weaknesses, it is time to prepare for Behavior Descriptive Interview (BDI) questions. Recruiters and/or interviewers, especially in big companies, tend to use BDI questions. These questions ask you to identify a time when something happened and explain how you handled it. For example, your interviewer might ask, "Tell me about a time when you felt really stressed at work. What was going on and what did you do about it?"

Additional general examples:

> Tell me about a time when you made a big mistake at work. What happened to cause this mistake? How did you handle it? How did your company handle it?

Tell me about a time when you handled a difficult client. Why was this client so difficult? How did you handle this?

Tell me about a time when you had to collaborate with others. How did this come about? How did you handle this? Do you like to collaborate with others? Or, would you prefer to work on your own?

Tell me about a time when you missed a deadline. Why did you miss the deadline? How did you fix this?

Tell me about your busiest time you had in your last job. What did you do to prepare for this busy period? How did your preparations help you with the workload? Did your manager say anything about your ability to manage this extra work?

Every job has slack periods. Tell me about the last time you had free time in your current job. What did you do during this period? What did your manager expect you to do during this period? Did you seek out additional work to keep yourself busy?

Tell me about the type of work you find most satisfying. How often do you get to do this type of work?

Tell me about a time when you faced an ethical dilemma at work. What created this dilemma? How did you handle this?

Below are some job-specific examples:

Retail – Tell me about a time when a customer was quite angry. What happened to cause this? What did you do about this? How did you feel about this situation? Is there anything you would do differently in the future if this happened again?

Management – Tell me about a time when you had to fire an employee. What led to this? How did you handle it?

Commissioned Salesperson – Tell me about a time when you missed your sales target. What caused you to miss this target? What did you do about this? What did your company do about this?

Project Manager – Tell me about a time when one of your projects experienced scope creep. How did this come about? What did you do about it? Did you finally get the project back on track? What was the impact to the organization of this situation?

Computer Programmer – Users sometimes come to you requesting you create a program without them having any concrete idea about what the program should do. Tell me about a time when you were able to help the user define what he or she needed and then created a program to meet those needs. How did you help the user come up with concrete needs? What did you find frustrating about this situation? What did you find satisfying about this situation? How often do you face this type of situation?

Nurse – Sometimes it gets so busy that following routine policies seem to get in the way. Tell me about a time that you ignored routine policies in order to get the work done. What led to this happening? What policy did your ignore? What impact did this have on your patients or colleagues? What did your supervisor say?

STEP 3:

Preparing For the Interview

F. Prepare Questions to Ask in the Interview

Prepare some questions to ask in the interview. An interview is a two-way conversation. Even if you are desperate for this job and you would take it no matter what the company is like, you have the right to ask questions. Asking questions does several things. First, it shows that you are prepared. Second, it shows that you are organized. Third, it will stand out in the interviewer's mind because few, if any, of the other candidates will ask questions. And finally, it will give you information about the company that you won't get anywhere else.

Write these questions out ahead of time, at home. Write them out or type them on an 8.5" x 11" sheet of paper. Put the sheet of paper in an 8.5" x 11" file folder and carry that in with you into the interview.

What do you want to know about the company? Some great questions to ask the interviewer are:

> How would you describe the culture at (company name)?
>
> What is the definition of success for (your position) at (company name)?
>
> **This question above will really impress your interviewer. He or she may not even have an answer for this since likely no one has ever asked this question before.
>
> What would the current employees of (company name) say about working here?
>
> What would previous employees of (company name) say about working here?
>
> What is the average length of time people stay with (company name)?
>
> How long have you (interviewer) been working for this company? What do you like about working with this company? What do you dislike about working here?
>
> Who would the person in this position report to? How long have they been with the company?

How long have they been in their current position?

Is this a newly created position? If so, what prompted the need for this position?

What are the opportunities for promotion and advancement?

Describe a typical day for this position.

Is the company expecting to do any layoffs in the near future?

Have 5 or 6 questions written down or typed out in advance on your sheet of paper.

When the interviewer asks you if you have any questions, pull out your written questions and ask them. It is okay to read them off your paper, one at a time of course, allowing your interviewer to answer each question.

STEP 3:

Preparing For the Interview

G. What is Your Vision For Your Career?

Your interviewer will likely ask you the questions: "Where do you want to be in your career in one year? What do you see yourself doing 5 years from now? How does your vision fit with this position?" You need to have an answer for these questions.

 I hated these questions whenever I went for an interview. I had no idea what I wanted to do a year from that point in time and definitely didn't have a vision for my career over a 5 year period. You might be feeling the same way. However, since your interviewer is likely to ask these questions, you need to have an answer.

 These questions are really asking three things. First, do you have a vision for yourself and your career? Second, how does that vision fit in with this organization and this position you are currently interviewing for? Most companies don't want to hire you for a full-time position if they know that you are going to be gone in a year pursuing the next big thing. The third thing this question is really asking is whether you have ambitions and if these ambitions are achievable in that time frame or are completely unrealistic. If you just graduated from high school or you just received your college diploma or university degree and you are applying for your first job, telling your interviewer that you expect to be president of the company in 5 years is completely unrealistic. The person interviewing you is going to think that you are arrogant and entitled and isn't going to take you seriously.

Scientists have determined that "mastery" takes about 10,000 hours of doing, practice or experience. Mastery is defined as being able to do something well without having to think about how you do it. For example, if you are a first year litigator, this means that 10,000 hours of courtroom preparation and litigating will bring you to the point of being able to litigate well without having to think about how you make this happen. However, you aren't going to know enough or have the skills to be a judge in the first 5 years of your career. If you are a first time manager, 10,000 hours of managing your human resources, material resources, budgets, planning and whatever else that encompasses your domain, will bring you to a place where you do this well without having to think about how to do this but this doesn't mean that you are now ready to run the company unless it is a small company.

The average person works about 2000 hours a year, give or take some hours. This means that it takes about 5 years to have mastery at something. Now obviously some jobs have less to learn and take less time to master but this 10,000 hour 'rule' is quite standard to master any kind of skill whether it is learning how to be an engineer or learning how to play golf. So, when the interviewer asks where do you want to be in 5 years or what path do you see your career taking in 5 years, think in terms of mastery.

For example, as an beginning nurse, what area of nursing do you want to gain mastery in? Or, if your goal is to become president and you are currently a manager, what areas do you need to master in order for that desire to come about? If you are just starting out and you don't have those 10,000 hours of experience/practice/doing, saying that you want to be Vice President next year has no credibility to it. It would be more productive for you to say that you want to develop mastery in your area of training, education and skills. It is also appropriate to say that you want to receive whatever professional designation you might be moving toward.

As part of your interview preparation, explore the question, "In what areas or ways do I want to gain mastery and how and where would that fit in the hiring company?"

If you are interviewing for a position that is a lateral move for you and you love what you do and have no desire to move up or around in the organization, state that. Let your interviewer know that you have mastery at being a _____ (sales person or mail clerk or receptionist or manager or lawyer or engineer or police officer or programmer or engineer or nurse (whatever your position is)), that you thrive in that role and that you intend to stay current on trends and research within that domain for the remainder of your career. Organizations need two types of people: people who love the work they do and want to continue doing that work at the same level; and people whom the company can groom and move around in the organization. Both are valuable and necessary for an organization's well-being.

Spend some time before going to your interview exploring which type of employee you are. If you are interviewing for this position because it will move you up from your current role, think about how those 10,000 hours (5 years) will be spent and what you desire to gain mastery in. If you are interviewing for a lateral position, even though you may already have mastery in your area, what else do you want to master within your role that will make you more valuable to the organization? What else do you want to master that will enrich your experience?

STEP 3:

Preparing For the Interview

H. Why Should We Hire You?

Why should we hire you? This question is really asking, "What sets you apart from everyone else we have interviewed?" The 'why should we hire you?' question is often a tough question to answer without sounding arrogant. There is a big difference between having confidence and sounding arrogant. Confidence is a knowing that you know what you know and that you are good at what you do. Confidence comes from mastery. Confidence activates a feeling of trust in others. When you are confident, people trust you. Arrogance, on the other hand, is often a cover-up for the lack of knowing, for the lack of mastery and a hope that no one will notice. Arrogance activates feelings of distrust in others and makes them feel unsafe around you. You need to go into your interview with confidence. Show your interviewer that you know what you know. Because you have reviewed your resume and you know what your strengths are and what your successes have been, it should be quite simple to point out how you will benefit this hiring company.

In addition to the above, you can also say something like, "I believe this is a great company and I am interested in what the company is doing. I am collaborative. I want others around me to succeed. I have brought tremendous value to my current employer in the following ways (identify what your achievements have been). I am really good at what I do and others can vouch for that. I own my voice. I speak up and share ideas. I am willing to speak out when things don't seem to be working properly. I will add value here." Obviously, if you can't say these things with sincerity or if they simply aren't true for you, then don't say them. No one will believe you anyway.

STEP 3:

Preparing For the Interview

I. Why Are You Interested in This Position?

This is a common question and quite frankly it is a question that every interviewer should want to ask you. This question actually encompasses a couple of questions. First, why are you looking to leave your current employer? Second, what is it about this position and this company that appeals to you?

I am pretty sure you have a very good idea why you want out of your current situation. Be careful how you answer this question. You don't want to trash your current employer. Although your interview is a confidential meeting, since everyone is connected to everyone these days, you never know who your interviewer knows or is related to. It really is best to say that you are looking for opportunities to grow and to contribute in a new way. If you can, say something positive about your current employer. If nothing else, that company is providing you with a paycheck.

To answer the second question, 'What is it about this position and this company that appeals to you?' reflect on the research you did on the company and mention something about that information that spoke to you. Perhaps the hiring company is having a particular challenge that your current employer went through recently. You could say that you understand that the hiring company is currently going through this challenge and that you have experience and knowledge which would benefit them and that sharing your new-found knowledge would be exciting for you. Or perhaps you discovered that the hiring company will be implementing a new technology or a new way of doing things and that you want to be a part of that.

You don't want to say you are interested in this position because you heard the company has a great benefits package/pays well/offers more vacation than other companies.

If you are currently unemployed, you can simply say that you are looking for work and this current position is a great match for your skills, knowledge and experience.

STEP 3:

Preparing For the Interview

J. What is Your Current Salary or Hourly Wage?

How much are you hoping to make in this position? Give this some thought before you go to your interview. If you are hoping to make a leap in your income from where you are at right now, answer this question in terms of what you want to be making. Think in terms of total compensation. This includes your salary or hourly wage, vacation time, health benefits, savings plan contributions, and bonuses. If you have time before your interview, do a bit of research on industry ranges. Women are still underpaid compared to men doing the exact same work. Claim your worth.

As a coach, it always amazes me how many people feel they aren't worth what they are being paid. I have a client who is excellent at what she does, and according to her manager, she is the top person in the company in that position. Given the education, knowledge, experience and performance of this woman, she is currently being underpaid. Unfortunately, this client read a salary survey recently that indicated that she was at the top end of salaries for the industry. This client does not believe that she is worth more or that a new employer would pay her more. This is such a shame. This woman is worth more than what she is earning right now but she has allowed herself to feel that she isn't worthy of more and because she saw this salary survey, she is convinced that she won't be paid more.

Be wary of salary surveys. These surveys are conducted by a consulting firm to find out what employers are paying for specific positions. The consulting firm will contact a number of companies, but not all companies, to get a range of salaries and benefits that are being paid and then the consulting firm will create salary ranges for job categories. There are several problems with this. First, it is in the employers' best interests to report lower salaries because this helps to keep employee expectations down. Second, it is often quite difficult to compare two exactly identical positions. This means that the consulting firm is collecting information on positions that may or may not be similar. Third, these surveys don't take into account whether the skillset being evaluated is in a growing industry or a declining industry. Finally, these surveys don't take into account the size of the company being surveyed and how many employees are responsible for getting a defined amount of work completed. As an example, a company with 10 people completing a set amount of work has a different stress and work level than a company of 4 people completing the same amount of work. All of these factors need to be taken into account when determining salaries. The value in a salary survey is to find out if you are being underpaid.

If your performance is mediocre you will be paid accordingly. If you do a great job in your work, you deserve to be compensated at a high level. If you are great at what you do, companies will pay for that. You need to go into your interview with the confidence that you are worth what you are asking. Just a note about this – there are limits. If you expect to be paid twice what you are making right now for the same position as you are doing right now, that probably isn't going to happen unless you are currently grossly underpaid.

Why should this hiring company pay you more than what you are earning right now? Simple answer – "I bring more value to (hiring company), having learned what I learned at my current company. I come to you with more knowledge and experience than I brought to my current employer. This is valuable to you (hiring company) and with increased value comes increased compensation."

If you are desperate for this job and you will take it no matter what it pays, you still want to claim your worth. Let your interviewer know what your compensation should be and that you will take it no matter what. You can say something like, "With the skills, experience and knowledge that I bring to this position, I should be paid (whatever amount you feel is appropriate). However, I really need this job and I am willing to take it for whatever it pays." It is okay to be honest. You might even find that the hiring company ends up paying you more than what was indicated in the interview all because you were confident in the value you will bring to this company.

If you work in an industry that uses pay grades or pay scales, it is important that you know what each pay grade or scale requires in terms of skills, education, and experience. Make sure that you are going to be paid properly based on your skills, education and experience. See if you can make a compelling case for moving up the scale.

STEP 3:

Preparing For the Interview

K. Prepare Your List of References

If the company is interested in hiring you after your interview, the interviewer will ask you for a list of references. You should have this list compiled ahead of time. Have a list of 3 or 4 references. Make sure that you have asked these individuals before your interview if they are willing to be references for you. Once your interview is over, contact these people again to let them know that the interviewer will be contacting them. Let these references know the company and the type of position you just interviewed for.

    Even though you will prepare your list of references ahead of your interview, don't hand out this list at the interview. At the end of the interview, when your interviewer asks for your references, let your interviewer know that you will email them to him or her shortly. Let your interviewer know that you feel it is important to contact your references again, as a courtesy, right after the interview, to let them know that your interviewer will be contacting them. You should email your reference list within an hour of your interview. If your interviewer is interested in hiring you, he or she will want to check your references as soon as possible. If you are slow in getting your reference list to your interviewer, he or she may start to wonder if you are serious about getting this job.

Who should you give as references? You want to give the names of people who have supervised or managed you and who have had the opportunity to review your work. If you are a recent grad, you could ask professors or summer/part time employment supervisors. If you don't really know any professors, you could ask your coach if you were involved in some kind of sport or organized activity. If you have volunteer experience, you could ask the person who organized your volunteer work.

If you are just starting out or are returning to work after an extended absence, you may need to think about where you completed tasks that someone else can vouch for and discuss. If you have been home with your kids for a while and you are now returning to the workplace, ask the teacher whose classroom you volunteered in to give you a reference. If you organized your kids' soccer club, ask parents who were actively involved in the club to give you a reference.

Really important point. This goes without saying but I will say it here anyway – only ask people to be a reference for you whom you know want the best for you. Don't ask someone to be a reference for you because he or she is the only person you can think of but this person has a grudge against you.

Generally speaking, interviewers do not expect you to give a reference from your current position, unless your current manager knows that you are looking around for a position that your current company can't offer you, or that you are being laid off. Interviewers know that it could jeopardize your current employment if you let your current manager know that you are interested in a change. If you quit your current job before getting your next job and you want to use your now recent manager as a reference, make sure that this person isn't angry at you for quitting. You don't need someone trying to sabotage your prospects for getting this job.

STEP 3:

Preparing For the Interview

L. Prepare Your Handshake

It seems that a lot of people have no idea whether they should offer a handshake at the interview, especially if you are a woman or if you are meeting with a woman. Go prepared to offer a handshake, regardless of the gender of the individual with whom you are meeting. If you aren't comfortable with a handshake, practice this at home. Ask your friends or family members to help you with this.

You want a firm handshake. As a woman, I am always amazed at how many people are afraid or are uncomfortable to shake my hand firmly. I don't want you to break my hand but I also don't want you to hand me a wet rag. As well, make sure that you have eye contact with the individual you are shaking hands with. If you practice this at home before your interview, it will be more natural upon meeting with your interviewer.

STEP 4:

What to Bring to the Interview and What Not to Bring to the Interview

What to Bring to the Interview

You want to bring a file folder and a pen with you to the interview. In this file folder you will have a copy of your resume printed out on white paper along with your written or typed interview questions. Even though we live in an electronic age, the workplace still runs on paper and having these two items, your resume and your list of questions, printed out on paper is more professional. If you have a briefcase, you can obviously put your file folder and pen in the briefcase and carry that into the interview. If you don't have a briefcase, simply carry your file folder with you in your hand. You can bring a small bottle of water in with you to your interview. If you have a cold, bring a small pack of tissues and a cough drop with you.

What NOT to Bring to the Interview

Strangely enough, lots of people don't think about the impression the interviewer will have of you if you drag lots of stuff with you to the interview. Here is a general list of what not to bring to your interview:

>Don't bring your gym bag to the interview.

>Don't bring your bike into the interview.

>Don't bring sporting equipment to your interview.

>Don't bring your sneakers, that you are going to change into after the interview, to the interview.

>Don't bring your lunch to the interview.

>Don't bring a snack to your interview.

>Don't bring your kids to the interview.

>Don't bring your parents to your interview. This actually happens these days. Don't do it. Even if this is your first interview ever and you feel quite terrified, leave your parents at home. Hiring companies want to hire an adult for the position and not someone who needs a parent with them to feel safer.

Don't bring chewing gum to your interview. Do not chew gum during your interview.

SECTION TWO:

The Interview

Before we get into the details of the interview, I want to bring up a really important point that few seem to think about. An interview is a two-way conversation and it is a two-way evaluation. Obviously, the interview is an opportunity for the hiring company to evaluate you. The interview is also an opportunity for you to evaluate the hiring company. Very few people regard an interview this way. Most people see an interview as an evaluation solely on the part of the hiring company.

As a candidate, you want to make sure that this is a company that you want to invest your personal energy in. Most people work 8 hours a day or more. This is a big chunk of your life and a big use of your energy. You want to make sure that this company is worthy of that. Even if you have been unemployed for a while and this is the only company hiring within a 300km radius, you still want to evaluate the company. If you have a better understanding of the company, including the negatives, you will feel more empowered when you start to work there. Also, if you find out that this company isn't some place that is worthy of your energy, you can then say no when the job is offered to you. When you go into an interview with the awareness that you are interviewing this company and not just that you are being interviewed, you will feel more confident.

STEP 5:

The Interview

Now that you have thought about an interview being a two-way evaluation, we will get into the details of the interview. If you have followed the steps listed above, this step is actually the easiest part of the process, even if it doesn't feel that way. At this point, you have researched the company. You are dressed and groomed properly. You have prepared for the interview. Having done this, you have met some of the critical generally accepted interview expectations and you will have started to build trust with your interviewer. If you haven't met these generally accepted interview expectations, your interviewer will start off the interview distrusting you, even if he or she isn't fully aware of why that feeling is present. The information below will help you present yourself in the best way possible.

Arrive Early. You want to arrive at your interview 15 to 20 minutes early. You don't have to go into the meeting place right away. Go in to your meeting place about 5 minutes ahead of your designated interview time and ask for the person you are meeting with. For the other 10 or 15 minutes prior, find a washroom and use it if you need to and check your appearance in the mirror. Make sure your hair is in place and that your makeup isn't smudged. Check your shoes to make sure there isn't any dirt on them. Make sure you look pulled together. Then use the remaining time as an opportunity to settle yourself. SECTION FOUR, at the end of this guide, is filled with simple energy processes that you can do/use before your interview to help get you into a calm, focused space.

Being on time for your interview is a generally accepted interview expectation. It starts to build trust. Being late for your interview is unacceptable unless some kind of emergency came up right beforehand. If you do face an emergency right before your scheduled interview time, call your interviewer and explain the situation. If you showed up late for an interview and you didn't have some kind of emergency that prevented you from getting there on time, I wouldn't hire you. If you can't make it on time for something as important as a job interview, what kind of trust will I have in you that you are going to get to work each day on time?

Getting stuck in traffic is not an emergency. You should plan on being stuck in traffic and leave early enough to get to your interview on time. Getting lost on your way there is not a suitable reason for being late. It shows that you aren't prepared.

Turn Your Phone OFF. You need to turn your phone off before your interview and place it in your purse. DO NOT touch it during the interview. Having your phone on the table is a strong and subconscious cue that you believe something more interesting or important will happen during your interview than your interview. If you came into an interview and placed your phone on the table, I wouldn't hire you. If your phone was in your purse, turned on, and it rang during an interview, I wouldn't hire you. If you sent a text during the interview, I wouldn't hire you. You need to show your interviewer that you are serious about this meeting and serious about the position. If you can't make it through a meeting without checking your phone, you are not going to get the job. Nothing is more important during your interview then impressing your interviewer with your focus and commitment to what is going on right there. Your friends, kids, videos of cute cats, and Twitter/Facebook updates can all wait until you have left the interview. Do not take your phone out from your purse until your interviewer has walked away after your interview has ended.

When you first meet your interviewer and whomever else might be participating in the interview, extend your right hand to offer a handshake to each individual. As you do that, look at the person and say,

"Hi, I'm (name). Nice to meet you." It doesn't matter what position you are interviewing for. Your interview is a business meeting. Treat it as such. A handshake is simple. Don't make it weird or complicated. A handshake does a couple of things. First, it establishes a level of professionalism, which is important. Second, it is a form of touch. Touch is important. It can reduce stress. It can set off the release of oxytocin, a hormone that helps create a sensation of trust and reduce levels of the stress hormone cortisol.

Most candidates going into an interview do not realize that the person you are meeting with, the interviewer, might be nervous just like you are. Even if the interviewer is a recruiter and meets with several candidates a day, each candidate is a stranger that the interviewer is meeting for the first time. Meeting strangers all day long can induce anxiety. In addition, if the interviewer is the hiring manager and hiring is a very small part of his or her job, then interviewing is an activity that this person does infrequently and is likely nerve-wracking for that individual. This brief touch then, in the form of a handshake, can help relax both you and your interviewer.

The beneficial effects of a handshake may be lost if you are meeting with a man. Lots of men are competitive with handshakes. So, instead of this being an opportunity for appropriate touch and the release of oxytocin, it can become a situation where you feel ambushed. If you feel ambushed by the person's handshake, simply tell yourself that you are okay and that there is nothing to feel unsafe about.

When you feel unsafe, adrenaline is released in the body, which causes you to feel more unsafe and your anxiety levels go up. The good thing about any non life-threatening situation is that once you start to feel unsafe, you have 6 to 8 seconds to react before adrenaline is released. During these 6 to 8 seconds, you actually have the ability to change your biochemistry. Pay attention to how you feel at this moment. Did this handshake make you feel unsafe? Acknowledge that to yourself and start to say words in your head that have a positive, safe feeling for you, like 'love' or 'joy'. Also, allow a little smile to form. Even if you are forcing this smile, your body will register this as a signal of safety. Doing these will prevent the release of adrenaline and prevent you from feeling more anxious and unsafe.

If you are meeting with a woman, use the handshake as an opportunity to form a connection. Most women don't use handshakes as 'power over you' actions so it will allow you the opportunity for appropriate touch and the potential to release oxytocin in both you and her.

An important note about handshaking – if you are sick, inform your interviewer that you don't want to shake his or her hand because you are feeling a bit under the weather and you don't want to spread this to them. Your interviewer will appreciate this. I know that I certainly appreciated someone withholding a handshake for this reason.

Once the interviewer indicates to you where to sit, sit down and pull out your file folder and a pen. As you will recall, this file has a copy of your resume as well as the questions that you wrote or typed out. Place both the file folder and the pen in front of you on the table you are sitting at. Open up the file and place your pen beside the open file. Your interviewer will be impressed with your professionalism. You aren't going to do anything with your resume. Having it simply makes you look organized and prepared. Having said that, however, if you are meeting with more than one person and the other people in your interview don't have a copy of your resume, you could hand your copy to them.

Be Fully Present. It is really important to be present with what is going on in your interview. You want to be focused on what your interviewer is saying and asking you. Being present means being in the here and now. It means your attention is on your interviewer and what is going on in the interview. Being present is a critical generally accepted interview expectation. There is such a lack of presence today. Presence shows respect and it builds trust. A lack of presence builds not only distrust but resentment as well. You don't want your interviewer wondering why he or she is wasting his or her time with you when you can't even be present during the interview. You need to be able to show your interviewer that you can stay focused on your interview for the entirety of it. If you are distracted while sitting in your interview, you aren't going to get the job.

Do not sit back fully in your chair. You want to look like you are interested in the meeting. Sit closer to the front of your chair and sit up, don't slouch and lean slightly forward. This tells your interviewer that you are paying attention to what he or she is saying and that you are engaged in the process. This increases your interviewer's trust in you.

Do not fiddle during the interview. Fiddling is distracting. It also underlines how nervous you are and it can get your interviewer wondering whether you are hiding something. And, since fiddling is an anxious activity, your fiddling might cause your interviewer to feel anxious. You don't want this. So, don't fiddle with the pen that you placed on the table. Don't fiddle with your clothes and don't fiddle with your hair.

Do not cross your arms during the interview. There are two main reasons for this. First, when you cross your arms, you give off the message that you are somewhat shut down and disinterested in what is going on. This can cause your interviewer to develop a sense of distrust with you. The second reason has to do with your own energy. When you cross your arms, you actually diminish the energy flowing in your body. You want your arms to be open. This keeps energy flowing in your body. Ideally, your arms should be beside you, either at your sides on the armrests of the chair you are sitting in or resting on your legs. You can also touch your fingertips together as your hands rest in your lap. This position is quite strengthening and you will feel stronger doing this.

Do not sit with one leg crossed over the other. Although this position looks elegant and can help you feel more together, it actually increases the level of anxiety within your body. There is a physiological reason for this. The vagus nerve, which is the longest nerve in the body, runs from your brain all the way down to your lower belly and breaks into a billion different nerve endings at this point. The vagus nerve is responsible for activating your parasympathetic nervous system which is the part of your nervous system responsible for calmness as well as other activities.

Men do best when the sympathetic nervous system is activated and adrenaline is released. As women, we do not thrive with adrenaline flowing through our bodies. We thrive best when oxytocin is flowing through our bodies. Oxytocin is released when the parasympathetic system is activated which occurs through the vagus nerve. When you cross your legs as a woman, you are cutting off the flow of the vagus nerve. Your brain interprets this as a warning sign that something is wrong and your brain will trigger the release of adrenaline. As a woman, with adrenaline flowing, you will have a harder time focusing on what you want to say. You will also feel more anxious and if you have enough adrenaline flowing, you will feel irritable. You will already have adrenaline flowing just by the very fact that you are in an interview. Don't make things worse for yourself by crossing your legs. Crossing your ankles is fine as is keeping both feet on the ground.

If your interviewer asks if you would like a coffee, say no and ask for a glass of water instead. If you have a small bottle of water with you, simply say you are fine. Even if you would really prefer a cup of coffee, if you are feeling nervous, the water will actually help you calm down whereas the coffee will increase your anxiety. Remember to be polite and say 'please' and 'thank you'. Manners go a long way in impressing people.

Try to remain calm. Even if getting or not getting this job means life or death for you, try to remember you are having a conversation with someone who invited you to be there. This person is interested in you, otherwise you wouldn't be there. As well, remember that you are interviewing them. My clients have found that by keeping this point in mind, they feel more powerful with the process. Also try to remember that the interviewer might be nervous, just like you are.

Take a deep breath. This will help settle you. Just a note about this – you aren't trying to blow up a balloon here. Just a simple, quiet deep inhale and exhale is all that is required. Try not to hold your breath during your interview. When we get nervous, we tend to hold our breath. This actually increases the amount of adrenaline in our bodies which increases our feelings of anxiety. It also makes it difficult to talk properly. Exhaling will help you calm down. Don't be weird about this. Just try to remind yourself to exhale and do it normally. You don't want to sound like you are giving birth.

Have eye contact with your interviewer and have eye contact with each person in the room with you (if there are others) as you answer the questions you are being asked. Some people like to avoid eye contact. I always found this to be annoying when I was interviewing someone. It feels disrespectful if you don't have eye contact. People want to be seen and acknowledged and your interviewer and anyone else in the room wants to feel seen by you just like you want to feel seen by them. Eye contact helps build trust. If you are shy, practice having eye contact with family members before your interview. Remember, this is eye contact. You aren't staring them down. Be natural about this.

Your gaze is important. Think about how your eyes feel. You don't want your eyes to have a hard look to them. This activates a sense of distrust in the other person. Instead, feel like you have a thread (not a rope) pulling the outside end of your eyebrows out gently to the sides. This relaxes the brows, forehead and the area around the eyes. Now, add a little spark of joy into your eyes. This will actually give your face a slight smile. This whole process will activate your hypothalamus, which is the hormone command center in your brain, to release oxytocin because it registers a sense of safety in you. When you are in an oxytocin state, you are in a physiological state of safety, calm, connection and consistency.

Your gaze affects your intercommunication with others. When your gaze is like what I just described above, it will actually activate the hypothalamus in the other person/people you are meeting with to register safety which allows a state of calm and connection to be established. In this state, you are establishing trust.

If you have young children or animal companions at home, practice your gaze with them. Young children and animals are highly responsive to the biochemical messages you are giving off. See if you notice any positive behavior changes in them. Also, practice this gaze on your colleagues at work. See if they respond more positively to you.

The good thing about gaze is that it can't be used to manipulate you or others. As you change your gaze, you change your biochemical response and the biochemical response in others around you. If you or someone else is trying to use gaze to manipulate others, your biochemistry won't be the right biochemistry to activate trust in others and their biochemistry won't be the right biochemistry to activate trust in you. It is like a sincerity meter. You can't fake this to gain someone's trust.

Answer your interviewer's questions the best you can and don't make stuff up. Just be yourself and be honest. This doesn't mean telling your deepest secrets. It just means sharing enough information about your work experiences so that your interviewer has a good sense of how you would fit into the organization. Try to feel joyful about sharing your experiences. Remember, you have successes on your resume that you have been invited in to discuss. Stay on point and don't ramble.

If you get to the end of your interview and the interviewer hasn't asked you if you have any questions say, "I would like to ask some questions." Take out your list of questions and ask them one at a time, giving your interviewer the opportunity to answer each question. If your interviewer hasn't given you any information on the company, start out by asking that person to tell you more about the company. You have the right, in an interview, to find out more about the company. Make sure you utilize this right.

At the end of the interview, the interviewer will generally ask you for a list of references. Let your interviewer know that you will **EMAIL** the list to him or her once you have informed your references that the interviewer will contact them. EMAIL is still the most common method of communication in the workplace and it provides for both a paper trail of the communication and a hard copy of the information, if required. Do not text your list of references.

There are three key reasons why you want to email your list of references instead of simply handing over your list to your interviewer at the end of your interview. First, you want to contact your references to let them know that your interviewer will be contacting them. This gives your references the opportunity to be prepared for this call. If your references are aware that they will be receiving a call from your interviewer, they will be able to give a better reference than if they were unaware of this call and were caught off guard by it. Contact your references right after your interview.

The second reason why you want to email your list of references to your interviewer is that it gives you a reason to send a follow-up email to him or her. More information on this is covered in SECTION THREE.

The final reason for emailing your reference list is that your interviewer will have it easily available when he or she goes to do your reference checks. Interviewers end up with piles of resumes and reference lists and it is easier for your interviewer to have this information in an email. Make sure when you send your email that the subject line of your email says, 'List of References for (your name)'. You want to **send this email within an hour of your interview** so you are still top of mind with your interviewer.

Make sure that you have your interviewer's email address before you leave the interview. If your interviewer didn't hand you his or her business card at the beginning of the interview, ask for one. If your interviewer doesn't have one available, simply ask for his or her email address. If you forget this during your interview, you can simply ask the receptionist for your interviewer's email address on your way out.

At the end of your interview, stand up and shake hands with each person in the room. Look at each person in the eye and say, "Thank you. I appreciate your time."

SECTION THREE:

After the Interview

STEP 6:

After the Interview

Within an hour of your interview ending, send a thank you EMAIL, not a text, to the interviewer and anyone else who may have been in the interview. Keep this short. Make sure you attach your list of references. In the subject line of your email type, 'List of References for (your name)'.

For the interviewer, write:

Dear _____, thank you very much for the interview today. I enjoyed meeting you and hearing about the position and your company. I appreciated your time. I believe I would be a great fit for that position. Attached is the list of references you had asked for.

Sincerely, (or Regards,)
Your Name

For anyone else in the interview, write the following to each individual:

Dear _____, thank you very much for the interview today. I enjoyed meeting you and hearing about the position and your company. I appreciated your time.

Sincerely, (or Regards,)
Your Name

Courtesy and appreciation go a long way. You might be the only person all day who has shown this to your interviewer and those in the interview. This one gesture alone might just land you the job.

SECTION FOUR:

Simple Energy Tips

This section contains simple tips that will help you remain calm during your interview. These tips may seem strange, weird or downright useless. There is scientific research behind each tip. Use the ones that make sense to you.

Interviews can be a stressful time for a variety of reasons. Stress is the feeling you get when you feel like you don't have the capacity to cope with what is going on. When you are energetically stronger, you simply feel better and you can handle the world more easily. When energy flows in your body better, you have a greater capacity to cope. As you increase your capacity to cope, your stress goes down. Wouldn't it be great to be able to thrive through your interview instead of just surviving it? If you did a few simple things that kept your energy and your vibration higher, you would feel much better physically, mentally, emotionally and spiritually.

Before your interview, play music that uplifts you. Music is very powerful and the right kind of music raises your energy. Any kind of music that makes you happy when you listen to it is beneficial. The exception to this is heavy metal music. Even if heavy metal makes you feel happy, it has a diminishing effect on the body. Masaru Emoto (The Hidden Messages in Water, 2004) demonstrated the powerful effect of music on water crystals and found the same to be true with the water in your body. Classical music, songs with a love theme (but not heartbreak), songs that generate a sense of community in whatever form all elevate your energy and your vibration. These all increase your sense of well-being.

Drink water. Water helps your body feel alive and full of energy. Drinking water helps the electrical system in your body to work properly. It helps your brain to function better and your muscles to fire correctly. Dehydration robs your body of precious energy. If you had a glass of water first thing in the morning before your interview, you would be able to think more clearly. Make sure that you are hydrated properly before your interview but don't drink so much right before your interview that you need a bathroom break in the middle of it. Sipping on water during your interview process will help keep you calmer and will help you mentally access your information more easily.

Turn your toes in. Whether you are walking to your interview or sitting in the interview, turn your toes in. Energy flows in circles. When the circuitry is intact, energy flows freely and reinforces itself making you stronger and healthier. When you turn your toes in, you keep the circuitry strong. When you turn your toes out, the energy drains out of you. Even if you are feeling overwhelmed as you sit down in your interview, you will feel stronger and calmer if you turn your toes in. If you keep your toes turned in during your interview, you will feel more confident. Just a note here – you aren't trying to rearrange your feet and ankles. Just turn your toes in a bit. It shouldn't hurt. If something hurts, you are turning in too much. Relax and be natural about this.

Circles make you stronger. By their very nature, circles are a continuous flow of energy and they make you stronger. Squares of any kind make you weaker. You can incorporate circles into your energy quite easily by doodling circles before your interview on a piece of paper or on your phone or even in the air. You could also wear a circle pendant necklace.

If you are in your interview and the energy in the room is tense, imagine thousands of circles floating down on your interviewer or group. I'm not a very visual person so actually "seeing" the circles is very hard for me. However, just by thinking of the circles floating down, I can feel the difference. This will shift the energy of the whole group. Do you feel like someone in the room is a bully? Imagine squares floating down on that person. Squares deplete energy and will take the power out of this person for awhile.

Put your tongue up on the roof of your mouth. This reconnects the main energy circuitry in the body. It also counteracts the weakening effect of pointing your toes out. Putting your tongue on the roof of your mouth is like turning on the master energy switch in your body. You can do this when your interviewer is speaking. Obviously, you want to speak naturally when it is your turn to do so.

Unify yourself. To stop your thoughts from being scattered or to eliminate the anxiety in your thoughts, you need to unify yourself. Concentrate on the area one inch below your belly button and think about nothing else for a moment. You can also do this by putting one finger gently on your belly button and one finger right below your belly button. With the finger right below your belly button, press in slightly. Keep that finger there while you breathe. Take a few breaths and slowly release your fingers. This will pull you into a unified force, quiet your mind and help you become more powerful. You can do this before your interview while you are waiting for your interviewer to meet you.

Use Rescue Remedy®. Rescue Remedy® is a stress remedy that was created by Dr. Edward Bach. Dr. Bach was a British physician who began to see disease as an end product or as a physical manifestation of unhappiness, fear and worry. He looked to nature to find healing flowers and created this emergency remedy. Rescue Remedy® is worth carrying with you in case of emergencies or everyday stress. Rescue® Remedy helps you go through difficult situations and stressful events such as an exam or job interview in a calm and relaxed matter.

You can carry the spray or liquid in your purse or jacket pocket and use it whenever you feel the need. Rescue Remedy® is inexpensive and can be purchased at health food stores or natural pharmacies. Use this before your interview, not during it.

As with all products, if you have a health condition, consult with your health practitioner first.

Get into your Right brain. Your left brain is full of the chatter that increases your stress. Your right brain is your creative center. When you are tapped into your right brain, your body relaxes and your mind chatter relaxes. You can get into your right brain quite easily. Doodling, especially lazy 8's (or the infinity sign) is a very simple way to access your right brain. You can doodle lazy eights around your eyes or you can doodle them on paper. You can do this while waiting to meet your interviewer. Singing a song, even in your head, will help you get into your right brain. If you can spend a few minutes outside, especially near some trees, before your interview, this will help you get into your right brain. And, walking will also help you get into your right brain.

Move your body. I don't mean do a big workout. No, I mean get up and move your body for a few minutes but not during your interview. Before you leave home for your interview, put on some music that really makes you want to dance. You don't want to build up a sweat but allow yourself to move to the music for a few minutes. The really great thing about this is that movement, of any kind, triggers your brain to release endorphins, or the feel good neurochemicals. You instantly feel better.

If you are feeling particularly stressed before you walk into the building where your interview will take place, running quickly in one spot for about 30 seconds will help you de-stress quickly.

Yawn. Yawning 10 times in a row is a very effective way to increase your level of relaxation. You will have to do a number of fake yawns to start with in order to do 10 yawns in a row. Doing 10 yawns will cool down an overly active frontal lobe which will help you become more effective at the task at hand (your interview). Research has found that this is more effective than doing 10 minutes of relaxation exercises. You can do this before going into your interview.

Put a hand over your heart area. Putting a hand over your heart area will activate the release of oxytocin in your body. Oxytocin is a hormone and it has the opposite effect on your body than adrenaline. Adrenaline activates your fight or flight response and oxytocin activates your tend and befriend response. Oxytocin calms you down and helps you feel safe. Place a hand over your heart area. Imagine you are breathing into the area that your hand is covering. Breathe in for 4 seconds and breathe out for 4 seconds. Don't hold your breath after you breathe in. With each in breath, say the word 'ease' to the count of 4. Exhale gently to the count of 4. You will notice a tremendous increase in peacefulness. Do this for a couple of minutes.

Laugh. Even though it may feel like there is nothing to laugh at, laughing is an incredibly powerful way to change your state of being. You may have to make a strong intention to laugh, especially if you really feel like there is nothing to laugh at. Laugh on your way to your interview. This will raise your energy level. It will increase oxygen to your body. It will help calm you down. Obviously, you don't want to break out into laughter during your interview, unless your interviewer intentionally says something funny.

Have some fun. This is really important and often forgotten. As adults, we forget the value of having fun. Have some fun with your interview preparation. Try to be lighthearted about this whole process. Think about something fun that you can do after your interview. Having something fun to look forward to after your interview can make the whole experience less intense.

Have this list with you on your phone or on a piece of paper. If you find yourself getting stressed before your interview, pull out the list and see which tips you can do right then and there. You can:

    Drink some water.

    Turn your toes in.

Imagine circles floating down on you.

Imagine circles floating on your interviewer.

Put your tongue on the roof of your mouth.

Unify yourself.

Give yourself a spray or take a few drops of Rescue Remedy®.

Doodle lazy 8's in the air or over your eyes.

Run in place for 30 seconds.

Yawn.

Place your hand over your heart area and breathe ease into your heart area.

You will be amazed at how well you feel energetically when you do these simple actions. Keeping your personal energy strong is the key to thriving in any situation. You can use any or all of the tips throughout your regular day and not just for your interview. You can teach these to your friends and your kids to help them have more energy, be more centered and feel more powerful.

FINAL WORD

Use the information presented in this guide as a way of getting to know yourself better. Use it to help you see how strong you are. Use the process of preparing for your interview as an opportunity to celebrate your successes.

As women, we generally don't allow ourselves the time to celebrate the successes we have had. We simply jump from one thing to the next without giving ourselves the opportunity to savor our success. The problem with this is that we never feel like we have achieved anything.

The mind has a way of making us believe that where we are right now is where we started from. This is untrue. Where you are right now is likely quite a bit ahead of your starting point. Perhaps you just graduated from high school, college or university and this is your first full-time position that you are interviewing for. Taking the time to celebrate your graduation success is important. A few years from now, it will seem like that achievement was not very relevant to where you are today. Or perhaps, as part of the interview preparation, you reflected on a job you had while you were going through a devastating divorce. Allow yourself to see how much you have grown and the strength it took to move forward. Allow yourself to celebrate the fact that you got up each day and went to work.

As women, we don't tend to look at ourselves and say, "Wow, wasn't I wonderful. I really made a difference. The company was lucky to have me as an employee." Instead, we pick ourselves apart and look for things that didn't go well. Stop doing that. You are harming yourself when you do that. That kind of behavior is abusive and it keeps your stress response always activated. Celebrating your successes, by yourself or with others, causes your brain to release dopamine. Dopamine is a pleasure hormone. When dopamine is released it creates a feeling that success is possible and it keeps you motivated to create more success. The more you celebrate each step of your success, the more often your brain releases dopamine. The more often your brain releases dopamine, the greater amount of dopamine gets released each time. This leads to consistency in action.

Just a note about celebrating your successes – you don't want to celebrate in an elated kind of way. Elation in women activates adrenaline. Instead, you want to celebrate your successes in a calm manner. You want to say out loud, to yourself or in the company of others, "Mmmm, that was good," as though you were savoring your favorite food. This is enough to activate the release of dopamine and prevent you from activating the release of adrenaline.

I wish you all the best with your interview. You deserve to share your experiences, background and successes in a confident manner. You deserve to have work that pleases you and builds you up.

REFERENCES

Emoto, M. (2004). The hidden messages in water. Hillsboro, Oregon: Beyond Words Publishing, Inc. Translated by David A. Thayne.

Index

Adrenaline 87, 90, 91, 92

BDI 49 - 52
Behavior Descriptive
    Interview Questions
    49 - 52
Be present 88
Biochemistry 11, 87, 93
Boundaries 43 - 45
Building trust 11, 12, 31, 47,
    61, 83, 84, 86, 88, 89, 92,
    93, 94

Cellphone 85
Circles 104, 105, 110
Clothing 21 – 23
Confidence 32, 34, 47, 61, 67
Creating distrust 12, 31, 61,
    88, 89, 92
Cross your arms 89

Dopamine 112 - 113
Drink water 91, 104, 109

Energy 9, 27, 81, 84, 89, 103,
    104, 105, 109, 110
Energy processes 84, 103 -
    110
Expectations 11, 12, 21, 83

Fragrance 24 – 25

Gaze 92 - 94
Generally accepted
    interview expectations
    11, 12, 21, 83

Hair 24
Hand over your heart 108,
    110
Handshake 73, 85 – 87
Hmm, I wonder 17, 18, 19,
    34, 37

Intention 27 - 29
Interview expectations 11,
    12, 21, 83
Interview *Def* 10

Jewelry 24

Laugh 109
Lazy 8's 107, 110
Legs crossed 90 – 91
Look polished 23 - 24

Makeup 23 - 24
Mastery 58 – 60
Move your body 107
Multi-tasker 42, 45 – 46
Music 103

Nails 23

Owning your voice 42, 46 - 47
Oxytocin 86, 87, 90, 93

People-pleaser 42, 43 – 45
Perfectionism 42 - 43
Phone 85

Research 15, 16, 18, 19, 60, 64, 65
Rescue Remedy 106, 110
Right brain 17, 37, 107

Salary surveys 66 - 67
Setting an intention 27 – 29

Shoes 23
Strengths 37 - 39, 49, 62
Stress 49, 86, 103, 106, 107, 108, 109, 112

Tongue on roof of mouth 105, 110
Turn your toes in 104, 109

Unify yourself 106, 110

Weaknesses 41 - 47, 49

Yawn 108, 110

www.ingramcontent.com/pod-product-compliance
Lightning Source LLC
Chambersburg PA
CBHW070540080426
42453CB00029B/788